D0363775

Other books by Exley:
The Fanatic's Guide to Golf   Golf a Celebration
Golf Quotations   The Crazy World of Golf
Golf Score Book   The World's Greatest Golf Cartoons
Golf Jokes   The Illustrated Golf Address Book

Published simultaneously in 1993 by Exley Publications in Great
Britain, and Exley Giftbooks in the USA.

12 11 10 9 8 7 6 5 4 3 2

Edited by Helen Exley
Border illustrations by Judith O'Dwyer

Copyright © Helen Exley 1993.
ISBN 1-85015-426-0

Pictures and quotations selected by Helen Exley.
Designed by Pinpoint Design.
Picture research by P. A. Goldberg and J. Clift/Image Select, London.
Typeset by Delta, Watford.
Printed and bound by Grafo, S.A., Bilbao, Spain.

Exley Publications Ltd, 16 Chalk Hill, Watford, Herts WD1 4BN,
United Kingdom.
Exley Giftbooks, 232 Madison Avenue, Suite 1206, New York,
NY 10016, USA.
Picture credits: Bridgeman Art Library, London: cover, title page
and, © Sarah Baddiel, page 60; The Image Bank: page 42;
Kunstegewerbemuseums, Zurich: page 27; © Sarah Fabian Baddiel,
Golfiana, London: pages 6, 8, 14, 20, 30, 34, 38, 39, 40, 46, 51, 52,
55, 56.

The GOLFER'S
ADDRESS BOOK

EDITED BY HELEN EXLEY

EXLEY
NEW YORK · WATFORD, UK

My handicap? Woods and irons.

CHRIS CODIROLI

I'd give up golf if I didn't have so many sweaters.

BOB HOPE, B.1904

B

_____

_____

_____

_____

_____

_____

_____

_____

_____

_____

_____

_____

_____

_____

_____

_____

B

My favourite shots are the practice swing and the conceded putt. The rest can never be mastered.

LORD ROBERTSON

C

_____

_____

_____

_____

_____

_____

_____

_____

_____

_____

_____

_____

_____

_____

_____

_____

_____

_____

D

*Water holes are sacrificial waters where you make
a steady gift of your pride and high-priced balls.*

TOMMY BOLT

F

H

The secret of missing a tree is to
aim straight at it.
MICHAEL GREEN

SAMADEN

18 HOLE GOLF LINKS
ENGADIN · 1728 m · SCHWEIZ

H

I/J

*I don't care to join any club that's prepared to
have me as a member.*

GROUCHO MARX

_I may be the only golfer never to have broken a putter, if you
don't count the one I twisted into a loop and threw into a bush._

L

M

I don't trust doctors. They are like golfers. Every one has a different answer to your problem.

SEVERIANO BALLESTEROS, B.1957

P/Q

P/Q

R

S

S

S

S

MOTOR

The Automotive ...er

July

50 C...

Edited by
RAY W. SHER...

A.D.A.
GOLF TOURNAMENT

*If you pick up a golfer and hold it close to your ear,
like a conch shell, and listen, you will hear an alibi.*

FRED BECK

I know I'm getting better at golf because I'm hitting fewer spectators.

GERALD R. FORD, B.1913

U/V/W

Golf is a game in which you yell fore, shoot six,
and write down five.

PAUL HARVEY

60e Année. N° 38   Le Numéro : 1 fr. 50   Samedi 23 Septembre 1922

LA VIE PARISIENNE

_____

_____

_____

_____

_____

_____

_____

_____

_____

_____

_____

_____

_____

_____

_____

X/Y/Z

Be funny on a golf course? Do I kid my best friend's mother about her heart condition?

PHIL SILVERS